Feeling Thankful

by Shelley Rotner and Sheila Kelly, EdD
photographs by Shelley Rotner

CAPSTONE PRESS
a capstone imprint

I'm thankful for **me**—

for the **things** that I have ...

and the things that I do.

I'm **thankful** for all the **people** who are special to me:

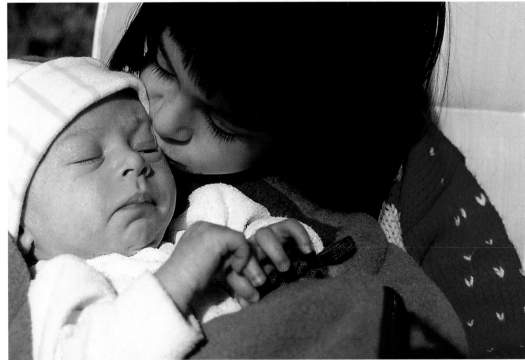

my family,

my friends,

and my teachers too.

13

I'm thankful
I have a **home**

14

and good **food** to eat.

I'm thankful for the **places** where I **play**.

I'm thankful for birds, butterflies, flowers, and trees.

I'm thankful
when I walk
in the rain.

I'm thankful for the **moon,**

and I'm thankful for the **sun.**

I'm **thankful** for the whole wide world.

A+ Books are published by Capstone Press,
1710 Roe Crest Drive, North Mankato, Minnesota 56003.
www.capstonepub.com

Library of Congress Cataloging-in-Publication Data
Rotner, Shelley.
  Feeling thankful / by Shelley Rotner and Sheila Kelly.
    p. cm. — (A+ books. Shelley Rotner's world.)
  Summary: "Full-color photographs and simple text illustrate a variety of basic things for which people are thankful"—
Provided by publisher.
  ISBN 978-1-62065-068-4 (library binding)
  ISBN 978-1-62065-752-2 (paperback)
  ISBN 978-1-4765-1347-8 (ebook PDF)
1. Gratitude—Juvenile literature. I. Kelly, Sheila M. II. Title.

BF575.G68R683 2013
179'.9—dc23   2012033987

Editorial Credits
Jill Kalz, editor; Heidi Thompson, designer; Wanda Winch, media researcher; Jennifer Walker, production specialist

Internet Sites

FactHound offers a safe, fun way to find Internet sites
related to this book. All of the sites on FactHound have
been researched by our staff.

Here's all you do:

Visit *www.facthound.com*

Type in this code: 9781620650684

Look for all the books in the series:

Different Kinds of Good-byes

Feeling Thankful

We All Do Something Well

What's Love?

Check out projects, games and lots more at
www.capstonekids.com

Printed in the United States of America in North Mankato, Minnesota.
092012   006933CGS13